MW00473922

BLACK · TAROT

An Ancestral Awakening Guidebook

....

Written by
NYASHA WILLIAMS

Illustrated by
KIMISHKA NAIDOO

RP **STUDIO**

PHILADELPHIA

RP Studio™
Hachette Book Group
1290 Avenue of the Americas, New York, NY 10104
www.runningpress.com
@Running_Press

Printed in China

First Edition: December 2022

Published by RP Studio, an imprint of Perseus Books, LLC, a subsidiary of Hachette Book Group, Inc. The RP Studio name and logo are trademarks of the Hachette Book Group.

The publisher is not responsible for websites (or their content) that are not owned by the publisher.

Design by Joanna Price
Illustrated by Kimishka Naidoo

ISBNs: 978-0-7624-7969-6

APS

10 9 8 7 6 5 4 3 2

For my Ancestors and spirit guides,
who are continuously paving the way.

To my soulmate Keegan, who loves me through all my cycles.

To Lucia, thank you for your eye and passion
for all unseen by the naked eye

—N.W.

....

Dear Nyasha Williams, author and creator of this deck,
You came to me with the idea of changing the narrative and
inspiring a whole new generation. You came to me seeing the
magic I could not see in myself. With every card we worked
on together, you inspired me to become a version of myself
that I never knew existed. Thank you for opening me up
to this platform of wonder.

—K.N.

CONTENTS

....

DECK STORY

I HAVE BEEN INTERESTED IN TAROT, ASTROLOGY, AND MAGIC from the moment I was able to read chapter books. Harry Potter, *Ella Enchanted*, and Artemis Fowl were favorites on my bookshelf. I have always dreamed of being a mermaid, so it's no surprise that water is my element. I like to believe that my Ancestors who were ripped from their homeland and shackled as cargo to a boat, who didn't make it ashore, transformed in their final breath to merfolk, gaining the power of the very element that swallowed them whole.

My spirituality has developed and evolved through unlearning and learning, decolonizing my mind and spirituality. I have been learning to embrace traditional spiritual practices that were taken from BIPOC communities, tribes, and groups. Many of our long-established spiritual practices have been demonized through colonization, the media, Hollywood, white supremacy, and under the guise of Christianity. We have significant work to do as a world to untrain ourselves—our minds, actions, and habits—from the lies and propaganda we have been fed for generations by those who currently hold power at the top. When I started with tarot, I believed that my answers came from my subconscious or my shadow self. Now that I have connected and aligned with my Ancestors and spirit guides, I know that any reading I am doing, be it for myself or others, comprises a message, guidance, and wisdom coming directly from them. Your Ancestors and spirit guides are always ready and willing to lead and protect you. You only have to ask. When I first began tarot, understanding and reading the cards took time. In wanting to strengthen and enhance communication between my guides and me, creating my own deck with imagery that resonated with me seemed like a logical choice.

Although I am passionate about divination, there were moments before my work on this deck was complete when I wasn't sure if I was the right person for the job. I felt as though I needed to know and understand more. Thankfully, many of my angels here on Earth (my husband especially) encouraged me to carry on with this creative endeavor. Self-doubt ultimately stems from being a beginner—both learning and healing take time, and our journeys are not always linear. Tarot is a visual representation of the many cycles of our lifetimes: trials, tribulations, and lessons. I hope that the cards bring you clarity and provide you answers, but if you still feel lost or in need of wisdom, slow down. There are answers all around you once you learn to take your time and pay attention.

I wish you all the love and peace on your spiritual journey. May you continue to stay grounded.

N. Williams

Understanding Tarot

There are times when we want a sign, answer, or message from the Divine in a format that is clear to read. This is where divination comes in. Divination is the use of various tools through ritual to connect with superior beings. It is a skill that takes practice, and it is recommended to find the type that works for you.

Types of divination include:

+ **tarot**
+ **automatic writing**
+ **runes**
+ **tea leaf reading**
+ **pendulum**
+ **osteomancy (bone reading)**
+ **lithomancy (stone reading)**
+ **scrying**
+ **numerology**

Tarot is a way of interacting with and communicating with the universe. We all have access to the Divine and to spirit guides who want to connect with us, provide wisdom, and advise us. They are always listening but can only engage and help us if we reach out. So call on the Divine and your spirit guides, tell them of your challenges, desires, and hopes, and make sure to ask for their assistance, intervention, or help.

The guides send signs to let us know of their presence. Signs can present in the form of:

+ **feathers**
+ **numbers (seeing the same numbers regularly)**
+ **clouds**
+ **scents (pleasant scents whose source you cannot identify)**
+ **music (being called to the same song or hearing the same song repeatedly)**

+ **rainbows**
+ **temperature changes (feeling cooler or warmer but not in an unpleasant way)**
+ **voices (a positive or parental voice in your mind)**
+ **advertisements such as billboards (a quote, word, or phrase)**

- light (sparks, a flash of light, shimmering without a source)
- dreams (which act as windows to the soul and mind; when dreaming, you are more receptive to receiving Divine messages)
- babies and pets (they are of pure intent and are often able to see more than meets basic sight)
- physical sensations (a light touch on your hand or arm, tingling on your crown)
- animals (through unexpected interactions, as each animal has a specific message or meaning)

WHAT TO ASK

Anything and everything. Any question or thought that weighs on your heart is a matter for your guides. I call on them about business decisions, conflicts in relationships, next steps to take—even whether a purchase or investment is a good idea. I have friends who call for advice when they are conflicted about an in-the-moment decision. The guides always deliver. Being spiritual beings, they can see so much more than we can understand or conceive. It is in our best interest to connect and build a relationship with them, to honor and show our appreciation of their guidance, and to call upon them in our hours of need.

Practice makes perfect. A card a day is a great start. Pull when you have a question or decision weighing on you. When I indulge in divination, I assure myself I am in a space with no distractions. With phone silenced, I open the window and use a cleansing tool (such as tobacco or spiritual waters) to clear energy in the space, allowing for clear messages and an overall better reading. Before engaging with any divination tool, I state my intent out loud: "Ancestors known and unknown, and spirit guides, I call upon you for your guidance and wisdom." I continue to call on them while I start preparing, shuffling, and holding the deck, thinking of the question I wish to have answered.

Black Tarot Deck and Guidebook

Water

The cure for anything is water: sweat, tears, or the sea.

Seventy-one percent of the Earth's surface is covered by water, and the human body is made up of approximately 60 percent water. Water carries and gives life. Nothing can exist without water. Its healing properties have been acknowledged by BIPOCs in their traditional practices and ways of life long before science could prove water's restorative properties. Water is often an essential part of spiritual enlightenment, and it is believed that water can hold memories created by sound, light, and human intention.

Growing up, I was involved in many water-related sports, including synchronized swimming and diving. As an empath, I feel most at home in the water; it helps me release any negative energy I absorb or pick up, allowing me to reconnect, purify, and restore myself.

Water is resilient, deep, and expansive; it ebbs and flows. My goal with this deck is to ensure that the traits of water are fully incorporated, so the Major Arcana all have water featured in the card imagery.

Moon

The moon has the power to move the tides, and that power extends to us, if only we tap into its energy. The moon embodies mighty feminine energy. It symbolizes birth, death, rebirth, renewal, wisdom, intuition, and spirituality.

The light of the moon is a reflection of the sun's light. Initially, I grew my understanding of the moon by following its cycles and reading about each unique lunar phase as it came to pass every month. I began exploring rituals for the full and new moon cycles, as well as the benefits and uses of moon water. (Moon water is water left outside under the moon, generally during a specific lunar phase, to be charged with the power of the moon.) The moon offers a time of effective and strong intention-setting, and its energy will boost the power of each intention.

Moon Phases

NEW MOON During this phase, the moon is positioned between the Earth and the sun. It cannot be seen from Earth. The new moon phase signifies new beginnings. The lack of light embodies the energy of a seed being planted, highlighting the possibility of something novel.

WAXING CRESCENT MOON During this phase, the moon has increased in size but is not half full yet. There is growth and the hope of more to come. The waxing crescent moon phase is a time of action and positivity. Set your intentions.

FIRST QUARTER MOON This phase, also known as the half moon, is a time of focus, determination, strength, decision-making, and commitment to action. During the half moon, focus on creative passions and put your energy toward completing tasks and goals.

WAXING GIBBOUS MOON During this phase, the moon is more than half full. The waxing gibbous moon phase signifies refinement. It is when you should work to refine and cultivate ideas and plans. It is a time for achievement and gain.

FULL MOON During this phase, the sun, moon, and Earth are all aligned, similar to their positions during the new moon phase, but the moon is fully illumined, being on the opposite side of the Earth from the sun. The full moon represents release and the sealing of intention. The plan is now in full bloom, indicating completion, transformation, fertility, and abundance. The full moon phase is ideal for letting go of anything that no longer serves you, including, but not limited to, jobs, relationships, thoughts, and feelings. Full moon energy can be intense and can come with a downside. The moon during this phase can enhance tension, increase heavy and intense thoughts, and encourage emotional behavior. Putting your thoughts and energy to paper can be a good way to relieve some of that energy.

Rituals for the Full Moon

Take a spiritual bath. Spiritual baths are used in many cultures to cleanse the soul, clear the mind, and ultimately heal with an intention. The goal is to remove any blockages that can get in the way of your growth.

Cleanse your (mental and physical) space.

Charge spiritual tools.

Meditate.

Dance.

WANING GIBBOUS During this phase, the moon's light decreases, but it is still more than half illuminated. The waning gibbous moon phase signifies gratitude. It is a time to work toward ridding yourself of bad habits, stress, and negative thinking. This moon brings about the energy of revelation, completion, and improved communication.

THIRD QUARTER During this phase, the moon appears half illuminated and half shadowed. It is the opposite of the first quarter moon. The third quarter moon phase hints at forgiveness. It is a time to pause, to contemplate, reevaluate, and reflect on the future. Take time to acknowledge accomplishments and prepare for new beginnings.

WANING CRESCENT During this phase, the moon's illumination continues to shrink. The waning crescent, in particular, signifies surrender. It indicates that the moon's cycle is coming to an end. It is best to detach from yourself and the world, to take time for rest. Ready yourself for a new beginning.

Certain special phases of the moon, such as the supermoon, the blue moon, and the blood moon, come with unique gifts and possibilities. I highly recommend using the moon's energy and influence to help set intentions and clear negativity.

Suits

Traditional tarot decks are made up of seventy-eight cards—
twenty-two Major Arcana cards (indicating major shifts or key themes)
and fifty-six Minor Arcana cards (indicating temporary or minor
illuminations)—that are divided into four suits. The deck contains 156
meanings if you choose to include reverse meanings. The cards are
based on seventy-eight archetypes: themes, images, and characters that
appear in folklore, myths, spirituality/religion, and stories across time
throughout the world. The traditional suits in tarot decks are Wands,
Cups, Swords, and Pentacles. Each suit is composed of four court
cards—Pages, Knights, Queens, and Kings—and ten number cards.
Every suit is linked to an element (air, water, fire, or earth).

In Black tarot, the suits are Wands, Baskets (Cups), Knives
(Swords), and Coins (Pentacles). Members of the family represent
the four court cards of each suit: Sons (Pages), Daughters (Knights),
Mothers (Queens), and Fathers (Kings).

WANDS

Themes: Goals, creativity, tasks, and inspiration
Astrological Signs: Aries, Leo, Sagittarius
Element: Fire
Traits: Social, public, and creative realms, where ideas
are turned into action; roles in family, community,
society; enthusiastic, energetic, creative

Themes: Celebration; emotions or feelings; relationships
Astrological Signs: Pisces, Cancer, Scorpio
Element: Water
Traits: Emotional and spiritual; love and healing; illuminate issues with creativity and understand sources of creativity

KNIVES

Themes: Observation, truth, and reason
Astrological Signs: Aquarius, Gemini, Libra
Element: Air
Traits: Action, rationality, clarity, objectivity; thoughts, ideas, beliefs; balance between intellect and power in intellectual pursuits

COINS

Themes: Home life, material items, and careers
Astrological Signs: Taurus, Virgo, Capricorn
Element: Earth
Traits: Wealth, security, protection; raw materials, money, resources, property, home, nature; commerce; workplace

Each number in the suits holds meaning:

ONE
Beginnings, Power Unity, Creation

TWO
Balance, Duality, Partnership, Choice

THREE
Creativity, Outcomes, Self-Expression

FOUR
Structure, Foundations, Hard work, Material Achievement

FIVE
Freedom, Change, Challenge, Uncertainty

SIX
Harmony, Love, Integration, Relationships

SEVEN
Tests, Metaphysics, Contemplation, Spirituality, Withdrawal

EIGHT
Abundance, Prosperity, Authority, Navigation, Manifestation

NINE
Conclusions, Completion, Achievement, Compassion

TEN
Beginnings and Endings, Infinity, Eternity, Cycles

Alignment (in Yang, in Yin, Aligning)

For every card, I have included the traits of the sign in yang (order) and in yin (chaos). I have also included guidance for aligning (how to get the energy represented by the card back into balance).

> **Yang:** "The known"—order, masculinity, day, authoritarianism, fascism

> **Yin:** "The unknown"—chaos, femininity, night, decadence, nihilism

Affirmations

Each Major Arcana card has an affirmation you can use to empower and embody the positive aspects of the card. The word "affirmation" comes from the Latin word *affirmare*, meaning "to make steady, confirm, and strengthen." Affirmations strengthen us, allowing us to build healthy minds.

Affirmations are a powerful way to reset and reformulate your thoughts, and the more regularly you call on them, the stronger they become. What we think, we become.

Our actions and reactions are often shaped by the daily experiences, conversations, and gossip that plant themselves like seeds in our subconscious. Living consciously requires reflection and taking the time to question our thoughts and impulses, whereas living unconsciously can create harm. We need to think before we act. Practicing daily affirmations helps us become more aware of ourselves. Conscious living is active, *positive* living.

Our perceptions of others are significantly influenced by literature and media—two of the central ways we gather information, interpret the world, and learn about people who are different from ourselves. The problem is that many representations are based on cultural stereotypes that tend to marginalize and caricature members of underserved populations, creating and perpetuating negative stereotypes. These so-called representations cause harm. We become limited, seeing a distorted view of others. Consistent exposure to such representations reinforces stereotypes in our psyche, making these seeds more readily available in our minds. We tend to develop self-critical habits that harm our self-esteem and confidence, lowering our resilience.

This is why affirmations are necessary. They teach us positive self-talk, training us to speak to ourselves with kindness and to pause before we react.

SPREADS

What do I need more/less of in my life?

What spiritual lesson do I need to master right now?

Where should I focus my attention currently?

What is the best way for me to bring more light and joy into the world?

How can I increase or find motivation to reach my goals?

What will help me find my inner strength?

What needs to be done to attract good karma and luck into my life?

What do I need to sacrifice to move forward?

How do I restore balance in my life?

What will help me heal right now?

TWO-CARD TAROT SPREADS

① Do	② Don't
Situation	Challenge
Blockage	Solution
Aim	Blockage
Ideal situation	What you are settling for

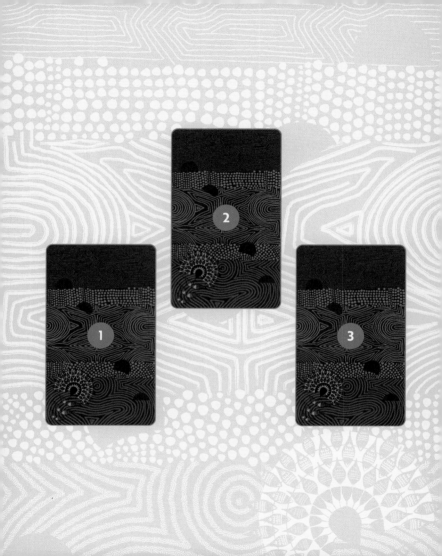

1	**2**	**3**
Past	Present	Future
Subconscious	Conscious	Higher conscious
Idea	Process	Aspiration
Mind	Body	Spirit
Physical state	Emotional state	Spiritual state
Option 1	Option 2	Option 3
What you think	What you feel	What you do
Worked well	Didn't work	Learnings
Strength	Weakness	Advice
What you want	What they want	Where it is going
Challenge	How to overcome	Goal
Release	Begin	Sustain
You	The other person	Your relationship
Where you are now	What is pulling you apart	What needs attention in the relationship
Your problem	The cause	The solution
What is helping you	What is holding you back	Your unrealized potential
Dream	Nightmare	Waking life
Ego	Higher self	Connection
Hidden talent	Obvious talent	Secret talent
Male energy	Female energy	How to balance my duality
You	Spirit guide	How to connect
Needs	Wants	Fears
Purify	Prepare	Allow to shine

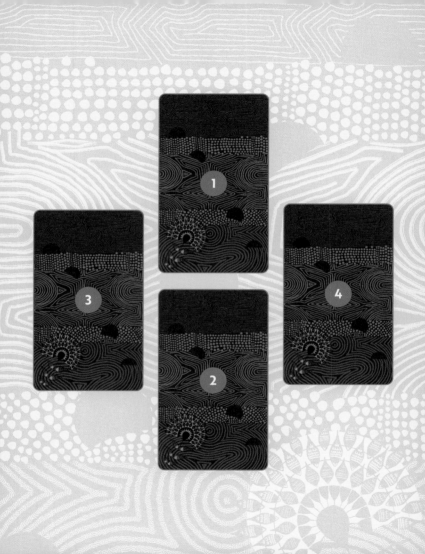

FOUR-CARD TAROT SPREADS

1	2	3	4
You	Partner	Hidden element	Illuminated dynamic
Current emotional and social well-being	What lessens my spirit?	How can I support my spirit?	What will strengthen my spirit?
What does my heart need?	How can I give my heart all it needs?	Who has a message of love for me?	What is the message of love?
Relationship's physical connection	Relationship's mental connection	Relationship's emotional connection	Relationship's spiritual connection
Situation	How you got here	Advice	Outcome
Soul	Body	Mind	Heart
New month theme	Past influences affecting new month	Roadblocks of the new month	Possibilities of the new month
North, earth. Possessions, finance, health.	East, fire. Desire, passion, personal.	South, air. Struggle, education, intellect.	West, water. Social, romance, relationships.
How do I energetically align with my desires?	Actions to take toward manifesting my desires	What must I master in order to be able to manifest my desires?	What will my desires manifest?
Lesson 1	Lesson 2	Lesson 3	Result from implementing lessons

FIVE-CARD TAROT SPREADS

1	2	3	4	5
Physical need	Safety need	Love and belonging need	Esteem need	Self-actualization need
Situation	What is serving you?	What is not serving you?	What obstacles are in your way?	Outcome
Career	Finances	Relationship/love	Family/friends	Spirituality/ well-being
Have I been cursed/hexed?	Reason for the curse/hex	Message from the Divine about the situation	How to remedy the situation	Final result
Problem in relationship	What I need in the relationship	What your partner needs in the relationship	How to find balance in the relationship or find a compromise	Final outcome
Something you overthink about	Someone you have been avoiding and need to address	An untruth about yourself you need to let go of	A part of your life you are struggling to understand	Something you would like to manifest in your life
Life path	Shadow	Past year	Present year	Next year
Your ability to receive/attract/ build money	Your earnings growth and potential	How you have handled finances/ money in the past	Blockages stopping your growth	Changes you need to make to move toward growth

SPECIALTY TAROT SPREAD

1	2	3	4	5	6
Which Ancestors are present?	What is their relationship to you?	What gifts have you inherited from them?	What are their hopes for you?	How can you honor your heritage?	Healing message from your Ancestors

1	2	3	4	5	6	7
Paternal bloodline blessing	Paternal bloodline challenge	Maternal bloodline blessing	Maternal bloodline challenge	Paternal talent to develop	Maternal talent to develop	How to maximize both talents

Immediate advice from your Ancestors	Additional advice from your Ancestors	How well are you currently aligned with your ancestral powers?
8	9	10

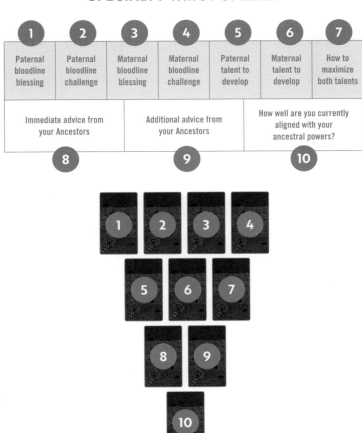

1	2	3	4	5	6
January	February	March	April	May	June
July	August	September	October	November	December
7	8	9	10	11	12

Preparing for a Reading

········· **GATHER YOUR DECK** ·········

There are tons of decks to choose from, all with different energy
and vibes based on the creator. Choosing a deck with artwork that
resonates with you is essential.

········· **SET THE MOOD** ·········

I like to start by cleansing my space and deck with smoke. Using
candles and choosing their colors based on your intention can generate
great energy. Do what you need to do to create a relaxed space.

SET INTENTION

Pause and consider what you would like to know. Speak your request out loud to the Divine, asking for guidance over what is weighing in your heart. The goals are to stay calm and focused, homing in on your intuition.

SHUFFLE THE CARDS

While shuffling the deck, think over your question. Handling the deck allows you to physically connect with the cards, letting them absorb your energy. Shuffle until you feel as though the deck is ready.

POSITION THE CARDS

Pull cards to match the spread you have chosen, placing them face down. (The more cards in the reading, the more in-depth the reading. For beginners, I would suggest starting with one- to three-card spreads.) Flip the cards over, and examine the illustrations before diving into individual card meanings. Pay attention to your emotions and feelings while looking for patterns and repetition in symbols, colors, numbers, and objects. Remember your reactions and observations as you dive deeper into the spread, reading the individual meanings.

Tarot—and all divination—can be an excellent way
to bring to light things we might be pushing under
the rug, or to receive help on an issue when we
can't see the complete picture. With practice and
time, you will get better and better at reading and
interpreting the meanings and messages.

CLOSE THE READING

Divination readings are a ritual and deserve the respect of a wrap-
up. Take time to meditate over the messages you received during
the ritual. Thank the Divine, Ancestors, spirit guides, and angels for
their assistance. Put away your tool in a safe space until further use.

CARD
MEANINGS

The Fool

The Magician

The High Priestess

The Empress

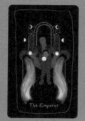

The Emperor

The Hierophant

The Lovers

The Chariot

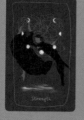

Strength

The Hermit

Wheel of Fortune

Justice

The Hanged Man

Death

Temperance

The Devil

MAJOR
ARCANA

THE FOOL

Traits: New beginnings, innocence, yes

Card Description: A young man is stepping into the unknown; it is a time of new beginnings. The daisies and wings behind him indicate innocence and purity.

The Fool symbolizes the alpha and omega, the unlimited potential we have at the outset of a journey. Being everything and nothing, the Fool acts on the pulls of creation, intuition, and impulse. Each of us starts our journey as the naive Fool, working, learning, and growing into our true selves by embodying every stage of the Major Arcana. We walk through the continuous cycle, eventually emerging as the enlightened Fool.

When the Fool card is pulled, it is time to consider the following:

- ✦ Are you living in the present?
- ✦ Are you ready to begin?
- ✦ What calls at your being to live out and achieve in your life?

Flower: Daisy (new beginnings, innocence, purity)

Element: Air

Chakra: Crown

In Yang: Innocence, adventure, a leap of faith, purity, cleansing, travel, change, excitement, opportunity, reinvigoration, vitality, possibility

In Yin: Naivete, lack of faith or hope, risky behavior, negligence, carelessness, apathy, distraction, impulsiveness, fear of the unknown, holding back, no common sense, immaturity

Aligning: Spend some time with the moon; journal.

Affirmation: I look before I leap, and I dare to follow my calling.

THE MAGICIAN

Traits: Action, power, yes

Card Description: A man stands on a rock at the edge of the ocean, and waves crash around him. His body is adorned with tattoos of the suits, the tools at his disposal. The suits honor the four directions and four elements. His presence in nature symbolizes his connection with inner consciousness and the outer world.

The Magician embodies the energy of manifestation, willpower, and determination; he is a conduit of both the material and spiritual realms. He is the reminder to turn dreams into reality, knowing you have anything you need to put your plan into action. All creation is possible with discipline, the most potent form of self-love.

When the Magician card is pulled, it is time to consider the following:

+ Do you have a plan? What is needed to live out your dream?
+ Are you using your skills, talents, and abilities to their full and most authentic potential?
+ Do you love yourself enough to give yourself everything you have ever wanted?

Flower: Gladiolus (power)
Element: Air
Chakras: Throat and solar plexus
In Yang: Manifestation, connection, action, inspiration, personal power, influence, resourcefulness, intellect, logic, ability, psychic abilities, commitment, bravery, comeback, spiritual development
In Yin: Poor planning, manipulation, greed, trickery, lack of clarity, cunning, self-doubt, deceitfulness, lying, cheating, traitorousness
Aligning: Explore new perspectives; break free of echo chambers.
Affirmation: I honor the universe, knowing that I have everything I need to succeed within me.

THE HIGH PRIESTESS

Traits: Slow down, intuition, yes
Card Description: A woman is submerged in a body of water, embracing all beneath the surface. She is the bridge and connector between the seen and unseen, conscious and subconscious, the light and the shadow. The pomegranates (the original "forbidden fruit") around her symbolize the secrets she holds, rebirth, and fertility. The two halves of the pomegranate remind us to balance all parts of ourselves: heart, mind, body, and spirit.

The High Priestess is the protector of the unconscious, reminding us to retreat and reflect. She invites us to the dream realm while also giving us access to earthly wisdom. She encourages us to find the equilibrium between opposites, like the cycles of seasons, or the sun and the moon. The High Priestess is the moon in all its phases.

When the High Priestess card is pulled, it is time to consider the following:
+ What do you need to allow yourself to *feel* rather than think about?
+ What is your understanding and relationship to intuition and the unseen?
+ Are you paying attention to your dreams and intuition?

Flower: Dahlia (balance)
Element: Water
Chakras: Third eye and sacral
In Yang: Mystery, spirituality, thirst for sacred knowledge, creativity, fertility, sensuality, common sense and wisdom, duality, the Divine
In Yin: Unwanted attention, blocked psychic powers, lack of self-belief, fertility issues, repression of intuition, indecision, stagnation, secrecy/deception, mental instability, personality disorders, herd mentality, gossip
Aligning: Listen to your intuition; vibe with positive people.
Affirmation: I trust in Divine timing, knowing all will be provided as needed.

THE EMPRESS

Traits: Grace, femininity, yes

Card Description: A woman is standing in a waterfall, basking in the water and nature. She is the cosmic maternal figure showcasing beauty and invincibility. Her femininity is expressed through nurturing, creativity, and sexuality, attracting what she desires.

The Empress carries the spirit of being alive, overcoming all fear, and living as her whole self. She is in charge of the sky and the Earth, reconnecting us with the mystic mind and our five senses. The Empress asks us to center nature and the wisdom of those who have come before us in our decisions and choices.

When the Empress card is pulled, it is time to consider the following:

- ✦ How am I taking time to restore inner balance in the chaos of the world?
- ✦ Do I accept compliments and abundance with grace?
- ✦ What aspects of life do I foster the most? What aspects need more fostering?

Flower: Water lily (fertility)

Element: Water

Chakras: Heart and sacral

In Yang: Nurturing, feminine power, abundance, motherhood, sensuality, spiritual rebirth, "birth" of a new idea, creativity, pregnancy, fertility

In Yin: Burnout, creative block, negative self-talk, neglect, insecurity, lack of recognition or appreciation, detachment from reality, emotional challenges

Aligning: Engage in talk therapy; practice daily self-love affirmations.

Affirmation: I welcome the wisdom and knowledge of my Ancestors, who want the best for my family and for me to heal and strengthen my family line.

THE EMPEROR

Traits: Solidity, structure, maybe

Card Description: A father sits on a throne with his son resting against him, comforted by his protector. He is the cosmic father, operating with the principles of authority, rationale, and order. He relies on these ideals to create stability and security.

The Emperor rules over the systems of law, discipline, strategy, and knowledge with paternal compassion and understanding. He protects and commands using a grounded mind and clear vision.

When the Emperor card is pulled, it is time to consider the following:

+ What kind of leader are you?
+ How do you show, use, and honor your power and strength?
+ How do you protect yourself and those you hold dear—physically, emotionally, mentally, and spiritually?

Flower: Red carnation (evolution)
Element: Fire
Chakras: Solar plexus and root
In Yang: Fatherhood, authority, structure, Divine masculinity, leadership, material power and protection, ambition, stability, rigidity, security, self-employment, opportunity
In Yin: Domination, toxic masculinity, rigidity, competitiveness, demand, offensiveness, power struggle, abuse, burnout, financial irresponsibility, health issues
Aligning: Set firm work-life boundaries; give yourself and others grace.
Affirmation: I speak my truth, taking a stand and acting on all that matters to me.

THE HIEROPHANT

Traits: Belief, tradition, maybe
Card Description: A woman is dressed in her Sunday best outside a place of worship. She operates as a seer, teacher, poet, and philosopher. She symbolizes the core values of learning rooted in structures and institutions. She honors the idea that all masters come from mentors.

The Hierophant imagery can evoke strong and dismissive emotions, depending on one's experiences with organized religion. A yogi, village elder, coach, therapist, and guru are some of the less conventional spiritual leaders that can represent the Hierophant.

While discernment when engaging with all institutions and systems is necessary, don't throw the baby out with the bathwater. Rules, regulations, and structure have their place in the world. The Hierophant divulges sacred wisdom and knowledge.

When the Hierophant card is pulled, it is time to consider the following:

- ✦ What aspects of what is expected of you could be good for you?
- ✦ What do you believe in or have faith in?
- ✦ What does tradition mean to you?

Flower: Anemone (protection against evil)

Element: Earth

Chakra: Throat

In Yang: Conformity, spiritual wisdom, religion, authority, convention, strict lifestyle commitment, ritual, immortality, conservatism, marriage, shared knowledge

In Yin: Morals, rebellion, personal beliefs, stagnation, challenging tradition, unconventional lifestyles, unconventional relationships, nonconformity

Aligning: Listen to or read a book.

Affirmation: I am open to receiving direction and wisdom from the guides, teachers, and elders in my community.

THE LOVERS

Traits: Unity, love, yes

Card Description: A couple standing in a body of water are about to kiss. They symbolize yin and yang, the union of opposites and the forces of desire and attraction. While the Lovers represent romance and love, this card can be representative of relationships outside a romantic context. It reminds us of the importance of self-love, and that honoring and understanding that love is the basis of an elevated and matured connection.

Ultimately, we all invest our time, energy, and attention in someone or something. The Lovers card asks us to reflect on whom and what we are giving ourselves to.

When the Lovers card is pulled, it is time to consider the following:

- ✦ Will your current attachments benefit and better you in terms of your long-term goals?
- ✦ How do you decide what to fully commit to?
- ✦ Is your investment in your relationships being reciprocated?

Flowers: Daisy, chrysanthemum (love)

Element: Air

Chakra: Heart

In Yang: Passion, harmony, love, relationships, soulmates, kindred spirits, perfect unions, desire, shared values, unity, opportunity, mutual attraction, healing of the heart

In Yin: Disharmony, imbalance, miscommunication, self-love, trust issues, conflict, disconnection, lack of accountability, detachment, emotional instability, temptation from unethical choices and opportunities, needed healing

Aligning: Practice shadow work and inner work; speak for yourself, not for your partner.

Affirmation: I attract relationships and connections with individuals that are in alignment with my higher self.

THE CHARIOT

Traits: Control, travel, yes

Card Description: A woman stands confidently in the bow of her boat. She is victorious in her goals, manifestations, and dreams because of her diligence. She understands that her determination and drive will guarantee success.

The Chariot calls you to buckle down and toil toward bringing your dreams to fruition. Her message is to remain focused and pay attention to details. It encourages finding your momentum, reminding you to navigate personal roads less traveled.

When the Chariot card is pulled, it is time to consider the following:

✦ Your success is assured, but will you take the leap?

✦ Are you "doing you"?

✦ Does your daily work build toward the world you believe in?

Flowers: Daisy, lilac (breakthrough)
Element: Water
Chakra: Solar plexus
In Yang: Action, conquest, control, success, determination, willpower, victory, investment in yourself, breakthrough, travel
In Yin: Self-discipline, opposition, lack of direction, patience, recklessness, slowing down, powerlessness, blockage, forcefulness, coercion
Aligning: Make a bucket list; celebrate the small wins.
Affirmation: I recognize opportunities that are in alignment with me. I utilize my talents and skills toward my success.

STRENGTH

Traits: Courage, strength, yes
Card Description: A woman communes with a panther, operating in a sustainable equilibrium with nature. It takes courage and power to act in accordance with your heart, mind, and soul. There is no true strength without love.

Strength is a reminder that if you stay grounded, you will triumph. She encourages you to be brave. You have what it takes to handle whatever comes your way.

The Strength card does not call for brute force but rather for a soft yet firm balance.

When the Strength card is pulled, it is time to consider the following:

+ Do you trust in your capabilities?
+ Are you ready to face the day?
+ Do you have the strength to show both yourself and others grace and compassion?

Flower: Peony (compassion)
Element: Fire
Chakra: Heart
In Yang: Courage, determination, persuasion, influence, bravery, overcoming self-doubt, perseverance
In Yin: Self-doubt, low energy, weakness, feelings of inadequacy
Aligning: Make a pilgrimage; master a new skill.
Affirmation: I am a fearless alchemist, able to transform all that is negative into that which is positive.

THE HERMIT

Traits: Guidance, solitude, maybe
Card Description: A man sits alone, realigning with the four elements and the ether. He knows the importance of taking time to retreat, as rest is revolutionary. We all need space for healing, growth, shadow/inner work, and decluttering the mind.

The Hermit can be a call for a retreat, pilgrimage, or adventure to sacred lands. He reminds us that we are both the guide and the seeker. An escape can be what we need to reconfigure our actions to be authentically planted in our truth.

When the Hermit card is pulled, it is time to consider the following:

- ✦ When is the last time you unplugged?
- ✦ Where do you find your answers—inside or outside yourself?
- ✦ Do you enjoy your own company?

Flower: Bird of paradise (freedom, joy, paradise)
Element: Earth
Chakra: Third eye
In Yang: The quest for enlightenment and knowledge, self-reflection, solitude, self-introspection, inner guidance
In Yin: Withdrawal, isolation, loneliness, materialism, bottled-up emotions, separation, reclusiveness, shyness or apprehension, avoidance of self-reflection, fixated/rigid/restricted views
Aligning: Do something that scares you; find your anchor.
Affirmation: I take time to understand myself, becoming more conscious and self-aware.

WHEEL OF FORTUNE

Traits: Karma, fate, yes
Card Description: A sunflower life cycle is centered around the elements, highlighting the phases of creation. The Wheel reminds

us to remain centered in a chaotic world. When you are centered, you surpass distractions and remain adaptable to anything that comes your way. The Wheel of Fortune says do not take anything for granted.

When the Wheel of Fortune card is pulled, it is time to consider the following:

+ Do you embrace aging?
+ What do you do regularly to recenter?
+ How do you break cycles of negative thoughts and habits?

Flower: Sunflower (longevity, vitality, good luck)

Elements: Fire and water

Chakra: Throat

In Yang: Good luck, karma, turning point, destiny, strong intuition, upcoming change, recovery, soulmates, decisive moments, breaking cycles

In Yin: Lousy luck, stagnation, chaotic energy, lost spark, impasse, neglect, upheaval, setbacks, disorder, external forces, unwelcome change

Aligning: Shift unexpected incidents into opportunities; embrace the unknown.

Affirmation: I align my faith with Divine timing; I surrender and trust the process and journey.

JUSTICE

Traits: Equity, truth, maybe

Card Description: A scale of justice holds water or life on either side. On one of the sides, a community of individuals works to keep the scales in balance. The collective's goal is to ensure that justice prevails. The Justice card is a sign of acting with integrity. Remember, every action has a reaction, so make decisions based in both compassion and logic.

When the Justice card is pulled, it is time to consider:
+ Do you take responsibility for the choices you make and the actions you take?
+ What do you consider to be truly just?
+ Do you call on empathy and understanding before making judgment calls?

Flower: Bluebell (humility, justice, consistency)
Element: Air
Chakra: Heart
In Yang: Truth, law, balance, fairness, thorough evaluation, karma, reevaluation of priorities, consequences, honesty, cause and effect
In Yin: Unreliability, deception, unfairness, karmic retribution, corruption, dishonesty, karmic avoidance, injustice, reparations

Aligning: Do physical labor; reflect on values and morals.
Affirmation: I am balanced and centered, continually working to create change.

THE HANGED MAN

Traits: Uncertainty, stalemate, maybe
Card Description: A woman is doing aerial yoga in nature. She is serene, embracing new concepts and perspectives within and outside herself. It is time for readjusting and recentering.

The Hanged Man asks you to surrender and accept the situation. She suggests that we lean into our intuition. Trust the process.

When the Hanged Man card is pulled, it is time to consider the following:

✦ When is the last time you made a worthy sacrifice for the greater good?

✦ Do you listen to your gut feelings?

✦ Do you allow yourself and others to change your/their mind?

Flower: Red poppy (remembrance, hope)
Element: Water
Chakra: Crown
In Yang: Letting go, pause, surrender, sacrifice, reassessment, new perspectives, release, uncertainty

In Yin: Indecision, stalling, delays, resistance, trouble, negative patterns and cycles, discontentment, detachment

Aligning: Take solo time; do a spiritual cleanse.

Affirmation: I choose patience and grace toward myself and others as we work toward our higher selves.

DEATH

Traits: Endings, transitions, no

Card Description: A child and a skeleton are in a garden, surrounded by greenery, taking care of the plants. Death is linked to fear—the fear of change and transformation. It is time to clear, cleanse, and declutter, allowing for the cycles of demise and rebirth.

The Death card indicates the need to abandon habits and end attachments. It is time for rebuilding, purification through deconstruction, and shedding. Death is the call to allow for new pathways.

When the Death card is pulled, it is time to consider the following:

+ Do you take the time to venerate or connect with your Ancestors?
+ Do you regularly check your ego?
+ Do you embrace change in all its forms?

Flowers: Daisy, lily (rebirth)
Element: Water
Chakra: Third eye
In Yang: Endings, change, transformation, transition, spiritual rebirth, new beginnings, letting go, end of one cycle of life for the beginning of another
In Yin: Repeating negative patterns, personal transformation, resistance, fear of beginnings, dependency, inability to move forward, financial crisis, dissatisfaction at work
Aligning: Create a list of your fears and then burn it; watch the sunset.
Affirmation: I embrace new beginnings and release all that no longer serves my good.

TEMPERANCE

Traits: Contentment, balance, yes
Card Description: A woman in a kitchen tempers chocolate, heating and cooling the chocolate to stabilize it, creating a glossy finish. She works to create balance, finding the perfect equilibrium. Tempering takes patience, understanding the gravity of a stable personal foundation, and collaboration with the community.

The Temperance card calls for moderation. Do not act in haste, as the material and spiritual aspects of a situation must be considered in equal measure.

When the Temperance card is pulled, it is time to consider the following:

- ✦ What do you bring to the table?
- ✦ Do you actively engage with viewpoints outside your echo chambers?
- ✦ Have you considered compromising?

Flower: Emilia or tasselflower (creativity)
Element: Fire
Chakra: Heart
In Yang: Balance, moderation, purpose, patience, calm, rationale, going with the flow, commitment, persistence, dedication, stability, tranquility, harmony, peace
In Yin: Excess, imbalance, hedonism, impulsiveness, negative behavior, discord, antagonism, clashing, lack of perspective
Aligning: Try a candle-gazing meditation; complete a project.
Affirmation: I open myself to focus on empowering beliefs that bring me closer to my full potential.

THE DEVIL

Traits: Desire, addiction, no
Card Description: A hooded figure wears a skull and has a spinning compass around his neck. He welcomes temptation in all its forms, pulling us in all directions. He embodies the ego, toxicity, and chaos

of the material world. Are you aware of all your addictions?

The Devil card means that it is time for an honest self-evaluation and for confrontation of our raw desires. He lets us know it is time to make peace with any fault, shame, or guilt we might be holding on to, and to forgive ourselves. We must face our demons.

When the Devil card is pulled, it is time to consider the following:

+ Do I act consciously, considering the law of attraction?
+ Do I choose to live in ignorance instead of facing the truth?
+ Am I giving my love, time, and energy to people and things that serve my betterment?

Flower: Apple blossom (temptation)

Element: Earth

Chakra: Root

In Yang: Attachment, shadow self, sexuality, addiction, negative attachments, focus on earthly pleasures, stagnation, feeling trapped, resentments, dangerous relationships, risk of clinical depression, risk of silent illnesses

In Yin: Dark thoughts, detachment, tyranny/narcissism, new awareness, financial troubles, working toward recovery from addiction or mental health issues

Aligning: Consume and indulge consciously.

Affirmation: I am in sync with my intuition and inner knowledge, which always lead me in the correct direction.

THE TOWER

Traits: Destruction, disruption, no

Card Description: A devastated shoreline is littered with trash; trees have been destroyed. Our world is in a dire state. Without strong protective action and time for healing (of ourselves and the planet), it will be impossible for the world to recover. The Tower serves as a warning of sudden change and the trauma that can come from it.

BIPOC communities worldwide have practiced Indigenous and traditional ways of living in symmetry with nature and her spirits, existing in harmony with the Earth for millennia. White supremacy, the patriarchy, and capitalism—political and economic systems that favor greed and consumption over a tradition of conservation and balance—have poisoned our planet. The old way is no longer viable; we can no longer live, eat, and interact without the health and stability of the environment in mind.

When the Tower card is pulled, it is time to consider the following:

+ Do you view your dollar as a vote toward the world you believe in?
+ Are you experiencing a breakthrough or a breakdown?
+ Can you see beyond your ivory tower?

Flower: Oleander (caution, destiny)

Element: Fire

Chakras: Solar plexus and root

In Yang: Upheaval, emotional strife, sudden change, revelation, chaos, disaster, unhealthy relationships, emptiness and loneliness, negative or hostile environment, failure/bankruptcy, vulnerability to disease, divorce, tragedy

In Yin: Fear of change, personal transformation, avoiding loss, delaying the inevitable, warnings of serious illness, averting disaster

Aligning: Realign with purpose; walk at night.

Affirmation: I am safe and divinely protected throughout all challenges I face.

THE STAR

Traits: Hope, blessings, yes

Card Description: A couple are freed of their shackles, joyously following the light from the North Star. The two are ready for the calm of freedom after the storm and the devastation of enslavement. They celebrate clarity after years of disillusionment. They have hope, knowing that everything they need is within them. Their gifts, abundance, and wisdom are all the sweeter for the struggles and challenges they endured.

The Star speaks to creativity and inspiration, asking how we can spread hope. The couple will need healing after overcoming a struggle (Tower energy). Take care of yourself mentally, emotionally, socially, and spiritually.

When the Star card is pulled, it is time to consider the following:

+ Do you remember when you wished, dreamed, and prayed for the things you have now?
+ Do you know your why? What motivates you to try again tomorrow?
+ Are you indeed free and authentically "you" in all circumstances?

Flower: Cotton flower (promise of wealth and well-being)
Element: Air
Chakra: Crown
In Yang: Faith, renewal, hope, spirituality, new opportunities, financial payoffs, inspiration, creativity, serenity, healing, positivity
In Yin: Despair, lack of faith, disconnection, pessimism, boredom, scraping by, monotony
Aligning: Paint; write a poem.
Affirmation: I draw and enjoy abundance in all forms with a heart of gratitude.

THE MOON

Traits: Clouded, unconscious, no
Card Description: A woman dances, honoring the light and dark aspects of herself. She knows her shadow is a part of her. She knows the importance of taking note of one's dreams. Now is the time to heed

our intuition to see through and steer clear of deceptions and illusions.

The Moon card brings to light any hidden truths and reminds us that the needs of our instincts (physical, emotional, and mental) must be met. She represents our journey through our inner shadows. It is time to make space for the waxing and waning cycles. Seek aid for clarity of the mind if you are experiencing depression or anxiety.

When the Moon card is pulled, it is time to consider the following:

+ Are you paying attention to warnings, signs, and visions?
+ What are you choosing to see, and what are you choosing to avoid?
+ What is causing you to lose sleep? What is affecting your health that you need to release?

Flower: Brugmansia (danger)
Element: Water
Chakra: Third eye
In Yang: Intuition, fear, illusion, subconsciousness, derailed plans, desire for change, hidden agendas, poor communication, poor mental state, dreams, anxiety, vagueness, insecurity
In Yin: Confusion, release, inner turmoil, pain subsiding, seeing true colors, creative lull, mental and emotional stability, truth, regained composure, blocked intuition
Aligning: Spend time in water; record your dreams.
Affirmation: I attract high vibrations, consciousness, and soul intelligence.

THE SUN

Traits: Abundance, fertility, yes

Card Description: A couple stand at the foot of a table, excitedly awaiting the addition to their family. They are taking time to celebrate life. The Sun symbolizes abundance and is a reminder of the law of receiving and giving: when you have more than you need, extend your table; don't build a higher fence.

The Sun card warms all it touches, reminding us of everything we have to gift to the world and to assist in spreading our light to others. Falsehoods of lack and scarcity were designed to divide us and to create imbalance with Mother Earth. We are encouraged to express and expand ourselves.

When the Sun card is pulled, it is time to consider the following:

✦ Are you searching for your dream life, or are you creating it?

✦ Who or what lights you up?

✦ When was the last time you took a break or a vacation?

Flower: Centaurea (fertility, hope, devotion)

Element: Fire

Chakra: Solar plexus

In Yang: Warmth, positivity, vitality, success, investment in yourself and in your endeavors, essential events, payoff, new interests, optimism, confidence, good luck

In Yin: Excessive optimism, naivete, inner child, blockage, being overshadowed by negativity, overconfidence, ego, pessimism, lack of motivation, oppression

Aligning: Root out any issues you have around trusting others; write out your life goals in the present tense.

Affirmation: I step into my power, sharing my light, glory, and jubilation with others.

JUDGMENT

Traits: Decisions, self-assessment, yes

Card Description: A spiritual guardian blows a horn, signaling danger after seeing two individuals struggling to stay afloat. Judgment is a call to step into our soul mission. It is time to transition from one state to another, becoming fully awake.

The Judgment card speaks of painful and challenging times. Struggles are rarely appreciated in their present moment. The card asks us to cleanse, purge, and renew in order to transcend.

When the Judgment card is pulled, it is time to consider the following:

- ✦ Are you able to ask for help?
- ✦ Do you hear your higher self calling?
- ✦ How can you absolve the shame and guilt you may be carrying and make amends?

Flower: Calendula (judgment, grief)
Element: Fire
Chakra: Crown
In Yang: Rebirth, awakening, inner calling, absolution, self-evaluation, composure, renewal, forgiveness
In Yin: Inner criticism, false accusations, ignored intuition, self-doubt, cycling karmic lessons, malicious gossip, blindness, indecisiveness
Aligning: Take a class; spend time in nature.
Affirmation: I value my energy, walking away from people, places, and situations that disempower me.

THE WORLD

Traits: Results, revel, yes
Card Description: A woman waters the world, knowing the importance of looking after the planet and honoring all living things. The World card indicates the completion of one journey and the beginning of a new one. It is the uniting of the outer and inner selves. The journey has forced us to confront, persist, and evolve.

Certain chapters must be wrapped up and brought to an end. Move on—the world and adventure await. Reminder: no one escapes judgment, not even the judge themselves.

When the World card is pulled, it is time to consider the following:

+ Are you liberated? Are you safe, grounded, and whole?
+ How do you show up in the world?
+ How can you heal the world?

Flowers: Daisy, daffodil (new beginnings)
Element: Earth
Chakra: Root
In Yang: Integration, sense of belonging, travel, accomplishment, completion, achievement, wholeness
In Yin: Delays, burden, disappointment, personal fulfillment, shortcuts, stagnation, lack of success
Aligning: Exercise; practice grounding yourself.
Affirmation: I breathe in and embody inner peace, embracing the calm of being connected with the universe in mind, body, and spirit.

Mother of wands

Father of wands

Daughter of wands

Son of wands

Mother of baskets

Father of baskets

Daughter of baskets

Son of baskets

Mother of knives

Father of knives

Daughter of knives

Son of knives

Mother of coins

Father of coins

FAMILY
COURT
CARDS

Daughter of coins

Son of coins

MOTHER OF WANDS

Traits: Passion, courage

Card Description: The Mother of Wands, depicted in a field of sunflowers, holds one of the blooms in her hand, showcasing her blossoming life force. Sunflowers always move to face the sun, reminding us to seek out light and, ultimately, truth. The sunflower she is holding covers half her face, an acknowledgment that not everyone will understand your walk and your journey but still it's important to live your authentic experience.

The Mother of Wands is willing to fight for what she believes in, no matter how uncomfortable or challenging it can be to stick to one's convictions. This card is a sign to allow your zest for life to color everything you do and to practice daily gratitude.

In Yang: Determination, fire, independence, entrepreneurship

In Yin: Jealousy, insecurity, maliciousness, gluttony

Aligning: Try something new.

FATHER OF WANDS

Traits: Visionary, leader

Card Description: A man is giving a presentation in a field, against a backdrop of the mountains. The Father of Wands embodies the fiery energy that comes with creating new strategies to replace old, outdated methods. He is ready to step up and take the lead when opportunities arise.

The Father of Wands can motivate others with his expansive energy. He is a reminder that success requires discipline and commitment. In a reading, this card highlights the importance of shaking things up and walking the unbeaten path, bringing your imagination and dreams to reality.

In Yang: Motivation, the big picture, wisdom, inspirational speaking

In Yin: Impulsiveness, ruthlessness, smooth talking, betrayal

Aligning: Make different choices around triggers and cycles.

DAUGHTER OF WANDS

Traits: Exploration, excitement

Card Description: A young woman stands in a busy train station, looking forward to the adventure that awaits her. Ready to take on whatever comes next, she carries the vibrant energy of an entrepreneur and warrior.

The Daughter of Wands is footloose and fancy-free. When this card appears in a reading, it is a call to action, a reminder that you will not be content sitting on the sidelines. The card reminds us of the power of travel and how much you can discover about yourself as you explore new places.

In Yang: Adventure, passion, reluctance to settle down, changes happening quickly

In Yin: Abuse, procrastination, irritability, recklessness

Aligning: Practice conscious eating.

SON OF WANDS

Traits: Energy, passion

Card Description: A young man is submerged in a glass tank of water while being circled by two crocodiles. A crowd watches as he records his daring experience. The Son of Wands recommends that you keep your eyes peeled for exciting openings that will feed your talents and dare you to be great.

This card is a call to take a risk, to give anything and everything a chance. It is time to start a new project or follow a different path and see where it takes you. Even though you may lack a plan and may be headed into unknown territory, you admire and embrace the potential.

In Yang: Fearlessness, exploration, solutions, healing

In Yin: Conflict, unreliability, impulsiveness, no boundaries

Aligning: Share one of your passions publicly.

MOTHER OF BASKETS

Traits: Compassion, calm

Card Description: A woman is shopping in a botanica or apothecary; she carries a baby in a basket on her back. The Mother of Baskets has a kind word for all and is someone to turn to for advice as she spits "mother's wit." Full of compassion, she is the reminder to give yourself and others grace.

The Mother of Baskets trusts her intuition and is tapped into others' energy, knowing what they are feeling and experiencing without needing to be told. This card is a call to respect and show reverence for all aspects of creation. She is a prompt to welcome any and all feelings, knowing that their complexity gives life its richness, meaning, and depth.

In Yang: Intuition (spiritual or psychic), fluidity, nurturing, healing

In Yin: Martyrdom, emotional instability, exhaustion, covert narcissism

Aligning: Send snail mail to a few loved ones.

FATHER OF BASKETS

Traits: Provider, support

Card Description: A man stands under an arch in his garden, filling his basket with some of the flourishing harvest. The Father of Baskets has a skilled level of emotional intelligence and carries this awareness as he interacts with the world. He holds the key to the equilibrium between the heart and the head.

This card in a reading is a reminder to hold firm to your boundaries and to voice your needs to protect your whole self. The Father of Baskets applies intellect, making wise decisions, not letting other people or circumstances distract him from his core values and morals. Remember: when you engage with others, you must practice peaceful navigation around their feelings and emotional triggers.

In Yang: Stability, generosity, resourcefulness, trustworthiness

In Yin: Manipulation, betrayal, hatred, insecurity

Aligning: Commit to volunteer work.

DAUGHTER OF BASKETS

Traits: Romance, idealist

Card Description: A woman walks forth into a lavender field, basket in hand. She advances with her heart on her sleeve, able to share her emotions without embarrassment or fear. She knows that voicing challenging and heavy feelings allows for healing.

The Daughter of Baskets symbolizes love in all forms: romantic, platonic, and familial. She holds the power to ignite and reignite adoration in relationships. This card is a sign to remind others of their magic when they have forgotten it; let them know they matter, are loved, and are worthy.

In Yang: Charm, inspiration, commitment, idealism

In Yin: Rejection, spiritual blocks, materialism, suppressed feelings

Aligning: Create a playlist.

SON OF BASKETS

Traits: New love, synchronicity

Card Description: A young man and his partner embrace on a bike, enjoying each other and the outdoors. At the beginning of their relationship, the couple is swept away by the romance of the honeymoon phase. They are naive to the emotional, spiritual, and mental trials they may endure as their union develops.

The Son of Baskets couple knows the importance of self-love, which, once mastered, will allow you to attract the companionship and attention you crave. The card sends the message to honor all parts of yourself and others, as there is much to be understood. Seize all the fresh emotions, and be kind to yourself and others.

In Yang: Dreamer, imagination, unexpected abundance, inspiring news

In Yin: Naivete, broken heart, depression, lack of discernment

Aligning: Upcycle an item.

MOTHER OF KNIVES

Traits: Truth, warrior

Card Description: A woman stands confidently with a knife in hand; behind her is the target on which she is practicing her throwing. She knows who she is and will not be easily fooled. The Mother of Knives is adaptable and carries wisdom gained from painful experiences; she is a survivor who has made peace with the mental, spiritual, emotional, and physical challenges she has faced.

The card holds the reminder to consider all narratives and their counters, to review all the facts. The Mother of Knives makes direct decisions and values unpretentious communication. She has confidence that she will come out on top in any situation with knowledge gleaned from past experiences.

In Yang: Witty, sets clear boundaries, forthright, perceptive

In Yin: Bitter, calculated, emotional manipulation, resentful

Aligning: Take a nature walk.

FATHER OF KNIVES

Traits: Intellect, dominance

Card Description: A man works to cut down a tree in a forest with an axe. The Father of Knives makes decisions with both his intellect and his intuition. He expresses himself with strong conviction. The Father of Knives works to balance ethics and morals, logic and reason.

He acts as a mediator, helping parties find opposite common ground. Able to win over communities and individuals by his equitability and objectivity, the Father of Knives is welcomed and well received. The card asks you to make decisions with complete imparity; make firm, well-researched resolutions.

In Yang: Ambitious, professional, truthful, ethical

In Yin: Dishonesty, prejudice, opinionated, hungry for power no matter the cost

Aligning: Read or listen to an "Own Voices" book or podcast.

DAUGHTER OF KNIVES

Traits: Passionate, opinionated

Card Description: A woman marches forward holding a knife fiercely in one hand. She is a woman on a mission and she will not be stopped. The Daughter of Knives moves headfirst toward her dreams and soul mission. You must focus to effectively channel this energy.

The card warns of allowing your determination in the climb toward advancement to cause you to operate blindly with the potential of harming others and communities. Make sure that while you boldly propel forward, your choices, your decisions, and the paths you take are in alignment with your true and highest self.

In Yang: Advocate, confrontation, reconciliation, inner work

In Yin: Ungrounded, condescending, chaos, poor judgment

Aligning: Plant a terrarium.

SON OF KNIVES

Traits: Gossip, antagonistic

Card Description: A young man dives headfirst into a body of water, spear in hand. The Son of Knives encompasses the energy of being wild and free. He has made peace with his fears and continues forward, ready to take on anything that comes his way.

The Son of Knives acts in bravery to the point of being reckless. The card reminds us of the necessity of voicing or speaking your truth. Assure that all ideas and thoughts are rooted in facts. Critical thinking is key; be teachable. Honor that change is brought by being open to new thought processes and ways of thinking.

In Yang: Clever, competitive, constructive criticism, mental energy

In Yin: Gossip, bad news, stalking, ghosting

Aligning: Get active and get your body moving.

MOTHER OF COINS

Traits: Generosity, opulence

Card Description: A beekeeper stands in an orchard on her honey farm, holding a frame from the beehive. The Mother of Coins nurtures a space of comfort as a loving host and soothing mentor. She is down-to-earth, resourceful, and bighearted, making all feel welcome and at home.

The Mother of Coins can always be called upon, especially in a pinch. The Mother's abundance is well earned, ensuring security and prosperity, which enable her to welcome more individuals to the table to enjoy her generosity. The card reminds you to show gratitude for all forms of opulence. Knowledge and health are riches she honors as generational wealth.

In Yang: Reaping fruits of labor, creature comforts, resourceful, honest

In Yin: Mismanaging, overthinking, blocking luck, bad investments, dependent, self-absorbed

Aligning: Do not spend for one week or month.

FATHER OF COINS

Traits: Economical, disciplined

Card Description: The Father of Coins stands in front of a table covered in cowrie shells. Behind him, his Ancestors are showcased on the wall. He (in a worldly and material sense) has "made it" and is financially secure. The Father of Coins knows that mindsets matter, and he has the ultimate abundance mindset, solidifying him and future generations.

The card serves as a warning to be wary of letting material security hold too much precedence. The Father of Coins as a protector and provider knows the value of wealth, as well as the burden it carries. Stay grounded while pursuing your aspirations. The Father of Coins immerses his goals and responsibilities in love. He is patient and consistent, working for the good of all and not just for his glory.

In Yang: Responsibility, heritage, receptiveness, wealth, security

In Yin: Poor money management, scamming, materialism, corruption

Aligning: Lead a service project.

DAUGHTER OF COINS

Traits: Diligent, thorough

Card Description: A young woman stands boldly, accompanied by her white mare. She knows there is work to be done but that slow and steady wins the race. The Daughter of Coins is prepared for setbacks, aware that falling off the horse is a possibility, but she won't be discouraged and is determined to climb back on the saddle. This card holds the energy of sticking it out for the long haul.

The Daughter of Coins revels in being dependable, building a life that supports her lifestyle. She spends her money wisely and always has resources for a rainy day. Be wary of becoming stagnant by being too practical, not embracing change, or avoiding risk-taking. The energy of the card can lean toward the extremes of being thriftless or hoarding, depending on how your energy flows.

In Yang: Focus on building finance or securing commitments, making proposals, advancing class size, gifts, new contracts

In Yin: Paralyzing perfectionism, wasted effort, self-worth issues blocking wealth and abundance, lack of planning

Aligning: Take a cooking class.

SON OF COINS

Traits: Persistence, manifest

Card Description: Two young men engage in capoeira on the beach. Capoeira carries the energy of survival, allowing its participants to remain psychologically, spiritually, and physically resilient. The Son of Coins works toward security and plenty with practical, driven, and patient precision.

The card is about dedication and determination toward your goals, but not putting life or yourself on the back burner in the process. The Son always finds a silver lining and enjoys sharing the light he sees with others. He knows that challenges, slipups, and mistakes are part of the process toward improvement and success. Be a dreamer and a doer.

In Yang: Ambition, solid goals, grounded, values education

In Yin: Obsessive-compulsive, debt prone, negative financial mindset, a parasite draining you

Aligning: Do Pilates or yoga.

Ace of wands

Two of wands

Three of wands

Four of wands

Five of wands

Six of wands

Seven of wands

Eight of wands

WANDS

Nine of wands

Ten of wands

ACE OF WANDS

Traits: Creativity, inspiration

Card Description: Two impala meet heads underneath a baobab tree in the savanna. Legend says that African royalty and elders chose the baobab tree as their meeting spot because they were able to commune with the spirits of that plant for guidance. The Ace of Wands is a call to heed your internal advice and wisdom. Be open to channeling inspiration and pursuing ideas that will allow you to rise above any obstacles in your way.

Act fast and harness Divine intervention when it strikes! This card is a green light to build the world and the life you believe in. It is sending you motivation to continue creating, making, and designing.

In Yang: Routine, spiritual awakening, a celebration of life, revaluation

In Yin: Negative reaction to revelations, energy vampire, narcissism, stagnation

Aligning: Read a picture book.

TWO OF WANDS

Traits: Discovery, progression

Card Description: A young woman sits in solitude at the top of a cliff. The Two of Wands symbolizes the plans you have put in place to reach your long-term goals—your manifestations put into action. You have the ability to choose and are well equipped to select the best path forward.

The Two of Wands represents the planning phase for the ideas you have been channeling. The route to fulfilling your vision of greatness comes into focus—you know where you want to go and what you must achieve. Power can be intoxicating, leading us away from our authentic intentions and desires. When this card is pulled, you are being asked if you are wielding your power wisely.

In Yang: Inner balance, material and spiritual equality, consciousness of self, care for environment and humanity

In Yin: Decision time, fear of change, acceleration of life/project/relationship

Aligning: Create a manifesto.

THREE OF WANDS

Traits: Expansion, foresight

Card Description: Three women lean against a fence, blowing bubbles. The Three of Wands, a card of peace, symbolizes trusting in the universe while pausing to detach from the material realms to gain perspective. The women are off the beaten path, hoping to discover all the opportunities that await. This card encourages manifesting, speaking your dreams, plans, and needs to the universe.

Tap into your vision for your world, and push past any limitations you have placed on your design for the future. Explore all the possibilities. Your thoughts and interactions are an energy exchange between you and the cosmos. Everything is connected; honor that network.

In Yang: Grounding and stability, actively choosing not to rush, trust mentality, in alignment

In Yin: Scarcity mindset, debt, delays, ungrounded and emotional instability

Aligning: Take the scenic route.

FOUR OF WANDS

Traits: Harmony, celebration

Card Description: A couple showcases their synchronicity through balance and strength while exercising and working together. The Four of Wands is about honoring your growth to this point. Stand back and look at how far you have come. The card is a call to celebrate all the little wins you've enjoyed throughout your lifelong voyage. Take pride in your growth, development, and alignment.

The couple lives their life confidently, knowing they are breaking generational curses, building roots and generational wealth—all while grounded in living authentically. They show appreciation to their Ancestors by creating a solid work-life balance and making time to rest in honor of those who were unable to in the past. Pause and take time to admire where you are in the moment. There are so many reasons to celebrate. Work can begin again tomorrow.

In Yang: Commitment, moving to a place to set roots, strong ancestral connection, home

In Yin: Problems and conflict within the immediate family, division in the community, sickness, money difficulties

Aligning: Host a neighborhood gathering.

FIVE OF WANDS

Traits: Conflict, rivalry

Card Description: A family of four are about to indulge in some ice cream. They are all reaching out to grab a cone for themselves, but the struggle is unnecessary because there is more than enough for everybody. Additional cones are prepped, and there is a full tub of ice cream on the counter. This card indicates conflict in which everyone gets scalded, but the fight wasn't necessary to begin with. Many disputes can be deescalated or avoided entirely by changing your perspective and acknowledging that the individuals or community you believe are your competition might not be the true enemy.

The Five of Wands suggests that you are being tested based on the inconveniences and delays of the day. Ultimately, don't fall for the bait. Not every situation deserves your time and energy.

In Yang: Diversity, revelation, common ground, competition, strife

In Yin: Leaving things that do not serve you, releasing control, jealousy, silencing your inner critic, taking control of the ego

Aligning: Challenge your virtual and physical echo chambers; listen to differing viewpoints.

SIX OF WANDS

Traits: Recognition, victory

Card Description: A woman sits on a horse on a carousel. She is victorious, basking in the fruits of her transformation through the cycles of life. The Six of Wands reminds us that our past does not dictate our future. Let go of any imposter syndrome that may be creating self-doubt. Share your magic with the world unapologetically.

Public recognition is wonderful when earned, but it should not operate as motivation. Success is still success even if not recognized by others. The Six of Wands is about owning and harnessing what makes you unique.

In Yang: Public recognition, completion of a cycle, growth of your craft, enjoying the fruits from the transformation after struggle, reconciliation and reunion in relationships

In Yin: Self-sabotage, dropping out and giving up, an accident, needing external validation

Aligning: Record your strengths and achievements daily.

SEVEN OF WANDS

Traits: Protection, challenge

Card Description: A woman smudges the air at a protest in front of armed forces. The Seven of Wands represents fighting for what you believe is just, defending yourself, and holding strong in establishing your boundaries. This card asks us to make decisions aligned with our inner being and truth, rather than coddling a wounded ego. Be your own activist!

The Seven of Wands reminds you of all the sacrifices, adaptation, and resilience required of your Ancestors for you to be where you are today. Call upon that energy and strength. Sweetgrass, tobacco, and cedar are traditional African American spiritual tools for cleansing one's self, space, and tools. The card encourages you to hold your ground; you will not be unseated. Make the choice not to compromise the best of you for anyone. Know your worth.

In Yang: Fighting injustice, multiple jobs and overworking, taking care of dependents, being the victim of attacks from numerous people

In Yin: Accepting one's limits, choosing between safety and health and what people expect from you, prioritizing one's health, being fired

Aligning: Make time to disconnect and cleanse.

EIGHT OF WANDS

Traits: Alignment, movement

Card Description: A young woman dances across a road with balloons in hand. This card reminds us to strike while the iron is hot. Pay attention to everything that comes your way. There is a ring of Divine timing to this card. The Eight of Wands indicates that an action is gaining momentum, thanks to your discipline and dedication to sharing your gifts with the world.

If you have a message to share with others, work to communicate your ideas confidently and clearly. The sky is bright and clear. You have persevered through difficulties, building a foundation that allows you to experience your best life. Harness this positive energy and excitement.

In Yang: Alignment with the universe, travel, protection, spiritual quest, job opportunities

In Yin: Accident while traveling or while in the house, deception, being left out in the cold because of selfishness, stagnation

Aligning: Explore or visit a new city.

NINE OF WANDS

Traits: Test of faith, resistance

Card Description: Nine individuals hold up the power fist as a united front. The Nine of Wands warns of the other side of consistent action: exhaustion and burnout. This card asks three things of you: defend yourself, persevere, and exhibit stamina. Whether you're fighting for your rights or exercising your voice, prepare for moments of discouragement, especially when the struggle has been ongoing.

This card is the sign not to give up. Enact regular spiritual protection for you, yours, and your spaces. Listen to your needs, and accommodate yourself accordingly. The Nine of Wands indicates a time to review and acknowledge your achievements and successes. Do not doubt yourself. Continue to fight the noble fight. Get in good trouble.

In Yang: Collective struggle, last stand, resilience, guarding your boundaries

In Yin: Exhaustion from drama and injustice, isolation, toxic relationships, narrow-mindedness

Aligning: Reflect and adjust your priorities.

TEN OF WANDS

Traits: Burden, responsibility

Card Description: A woman walks with a baby on her back, bags in her hands, and a pile of collected sticks on her head. She bears a heavy load and has an overwhelming number of commitments and responsibilities. The card carries humanitarian energy on an individual, community, or collective level. Although giving is an act of love our world needs, be wary of giving too much of yourself. Don't allow getting caught up in the hustle and bustle to become an excuse to hide from the things you'd rather not address or process.

The Ten of Wands reminds us to avoid becoming exploited in service to others. Whether the burden you are carrying is your own or others', it's essential to find a release. Ultimately, you must ensure that your cup is constantly being refilled, and that what you give out to the world can be sourced from the overflow of the saucer. Your cup must always be full. You are not your achievements and successes. Take time to savor life. Remember, rest is also revolutionary.

In Yang: End of economic struggle, bittersweet and liberating death, ending exploitation and abuse, release, self-care, taking time off

In Yin: Heading toward illness because of responsibilities, too much on your plate, having the impression you cannot do enough, unbalanced, no peace of mind, discrimination

Aligning: Spend time creating with people who inspire and uplift you.

Ace of baskets

Two of baskets

Three of baskets

Four of baskets

Five of baskets

Six of baskets

Seven of baskets

Eight of baskets

BASKETS

Nine of baskets

Ten of baskets

ACE OF BASKETS

Traits: Compassion, intimacy

Card Description: A man sits on a chair in a field of flowers, one of his Ancestors standing behind him with his hands on the seated man's shoulders. The man has been soul-searching, looking for his purpose. He has come to realize that what he longs for cannot be found outside of himself.

The Ace of Baskets carries the energy of emotional fulfillment. It indicates an overflow of abundance and peace. This card calls for you to live in a way that will build generational peace, compassion, and grace. It is time to welcome all that is blossoming and blooming.

In Yang: Spiritual beginning or awakening, new relationships, compassion, search within the soul for one's true purpose or desire

In Yin: Emptiness, emotional loss, repressed emotions, miscarriage

Aligning: Spoil yourself as you would a loved one.

TWO OF BASKETS

Traits: Mutual attraction, partnership

Card Description: A couple has planter boxes full of flowers that they are about to transplant to their garden. They have reached the point in their healing journey when a true partnership can grab root and they can start building their life together.

Both individuals can make solid decisions founded in love. This is what it means to be vulnerable, to be able to give freely, and to warmly accept and receive love. You must offer yourself wholly to the relationship and trust your partner to do the same. True intimacy means allowing oneself to truly be seen and knowing you are safe unadorned.

In Yang: Complete healing, functional daily life, service to humanity, true partnership (doctor and patient; teacher and student; romantic relationship)

In Yin: Disharmony, broken communication, breakups, tension

Aligning: Have a tech-free date day.

THREE OF BASKETS

Traits: Collaboration, support

Card Description: Three women rest on a blanket, enjoying grand food and grander company. They understand that one of the most significant forms of wealth is mutual support. The Three of Baskets is a call to celebrations and reunions. It is about reveling in wins on all levels.

It's time to give and receive, hold and be held, support and be supported. You are enough. You have always been enough. Allow yourself to be loved as you are and to love others as they are. Embrace the equitable exchange of giving a lot but also receiving a lot. The Three of Baskets asks you to focus on how your individual gifts can be amplified as a whole. Consider how you can celebrate others in mind, body, and spirit. Connect with a tribe that uplifts you. Take time to create space for sheer joy and love with others. Walk in alignment where all can prosper and flourish.

In Yang: Community, mutual support, prosperity, celebration

In Yin: Isolation, gossip, three's a crowd, harmful partying

Aligning: Pause to take note of who is in your circle and who's in your corner.

FOUR OF BASKETS

Traits: Reevaluation, contemplation

Card Description: A woman pauses to look in the mirror. She is feeling stuck. She looks away from the baskets, uninterested; she doesn't see the new growth in the plants on the wall, a sign of potential opportunity. She only has to look around to see it. The Four of Baskets represents the need to ground ourselves, reflect, and make a new choice. It is time to rekindle your imagination and curiosity.

The mirror is an ask that you look not only externally but internally. Where are your stress and struggles resonating from? Dwelling in the past or obsessing about the future steals you of the present. Previous hardships and heartbreak or distractions may be preventing you from seeing blessings and miracles. Step away from the cycles of worry and fear, as they lessen your ability to receive. This card is a call to shift your focus to what is working and to open yourself up for more good to come.

In Yang: Refusal to fall in love again or take another chance of being hurt, news about a situation that has already developed, a time of stability when you can begin to establish a relationship with yourself

In Yin: Realignment, withdrawal, depression, rejection of help

Aligning: Say yes to others who are offering to lend a hand.

FIVE OF BASKETS

Traits: Disappointment, loss

Card Description: A man has dropped cartons of eggs on the ground at a market. Although one carton is unsalvageable, four others are intact—but the man's focus is on the loss. Loss is painful. The Five of Baskets offers permission to grieve. Allow for a release, as all your emotions are valid. Part of the healing process involves mourning and processing. Remember that healing is not linear—some days, weeks, months, or years will be easier than others.

Avoiding things doesn't make them go away. Make space for being in your feelings, but don't make a home there. Not all is lost. Practice shifting your focus to joyous memories. You will feel happiness again. Trust that the best is yet to come.

In Yang: Dwelling on the negative and not appreciating what you have, loss of perspective, disappointment, regret

In Yin: Personal setbacks, feelings of abandonment, unwelcome change, emotional release

Aligning: Recite daily affirmations with intent.

SIX OF BASKETS

Traits: Nostalgia, innocence

Card Description: Two children are in a field, picking strawberries together. It is their first chance at a bit of independence while they wander the rows collecting and indulging in strawberries. The Six of Baskets is a call to simpler, kinder ways of living. It asks you to consider what really, really matters at the end of the day. Whatever the answer is, do more of it. Build in time for carefree moments.

Much of what makes life worthwhile is who is with us on our journey. Remember what a reciprocal relationship looks like? You sustain them, and they sustain you. Send and receive the message of support. This card screams to make time for things that set your soul alight. Be reminded of your heritage and how you can honor those aspects of your ancestry as you create your own roots.

In Yang: For better or worse, letting down your guard, untainted by preconception, visionary, nostalgia

In Yin: Living in the past, leaving home, childhood abuse, attachment to outdated beliefs

Aligning: Go on a picnic.

SEVEN OF BASKETS

Traits: Opportunities, illusion

Card Description: There are seven baskets in a market stall.

- Basket one represents love (pomegranate, lemon, chocolate, and honey).
- Basket two represents property (wood).
- Basket three represents wealth (pineapple).
- Basket four represents revenge (black roses).
- Basket five represents victory (victory-garden harvest).
- Basket six represents death (junk food).
- Basket seven represents our higher self, Ancestors, spirit guides, guardian angels (feathers and candles).

Each basket offers a different temptation. One, containing feathers and candles, offers a connection to your higher self and the Divine. Every other basket is tainted with ego, attachments, obsessions, cravings, and selfishness. Do you know what you really want? What is truly going to bring you peace? Choose wisely.

In Yang: Time to make a choice, multiple options, wishful thinking, visionary

In Yin: Overwhelmed by choices, romanticism, castles made of sand, avoidance of challenges or confrontation

Aligning: Do what scares you.

EIGHT OF BASKETS

Traits: Escapism, withdrawal

Card Description: A woman starts down a new path, leaving behind all her baggage. She knows she could sit and wallow in the emotions connected to the past that have led to this point. It takes courage to walk away and forge a new route. At times, we have to stop and admit to ourselves that things are no longer working and are unable to be mended.

It is not an easy decision to withdraw from someone or something that you have invested so much time, energy, and love into, but acknowledge that not everything is meant to last. The Eight of Baskets is about honoring what is meant for you and being able to freely say goodbye to all that no longer resonates. It is the most tenderhearted of breakups that, while difficult, is necessary. We cannot keep giving time, energy, and space to people and things that hurt us or hold us back. It's time to release the soul ties that are no longer serving you.

In Yang: Leaving the past behind, disappointment, seeking of truth, self-discovery

In Yin: Indecision, fear of the unknown, making regrettable choices, avoiding responsibilities

Aligning: Trust your gut feeling and make the change you have been putting off.

NINE OF BASKETS

Traits: Gratitude, contentment

Card Description: A couple dressed to the nines is standing outside, having just returned from a bucket-list trip. The couple hasn't reached total fulfillment, but things are good. They walk in comfort knowing their needs are met, their relationship has flow, and they've found peace. The Nine of Baskets hints at manifestations coming to fruition.

The card is also a reminder that you have always been enough and have always been worthy. Bask in the moment; fully appreciate your journey to this point. Claim satisfaction before you walk down the path of gluttony, greed, or ego. Your delight, contentment, pleasure, or peace should never feel like a show to impress, nor should you put up a facade of perfection if things are not great. You are safe. You have enough. You *are* enough.

In Yang: Dreams coming true, enjoying the finer things in life, financial security, experiencing your heart's desires, "coming on up"

In Yin: Unfulfillment, overindulgence/gluttony, shallowness/hedonism (a "front" to impress others), excessive pride

Aligning: Detach yourself from posting online about your peace for others to see; instead, be present in it.

TEN OF BASKETS

Traits: Happiness, alignment

Card Description: Family breaks bread together at a table; the hosts are fulfilled by being able to entertain and enjoy loved ones. This is a card of celebration, carrying the energy of joy, peace, contentment, family, and faith. The Ten of Baskets is the homecoming of emotional fulfillment. Your heart is home because you know who you are and what you are here on Earth to accomplish. You are welcomed and surrounded in love.

The wealth of food, company, and baskets is a showcase of abundant blessings. This card represents the solace of finding your family, who accept you and bring tranquility to your life. Remember to show love to those who see you and have stuck by you on your walk. Recognizing our interconnectedness with all that is brings joy and peace.

In Yang: Celebrations with loved ones, blessings, Divine love, blissful relationships

In Yin: Broken home, misaligned values, difficult and struggling relationships (toxic or abusive relatives or family members), empty nest

Aligning: Take your power back, realigning with the life you want to live.

Ace of Knives

Two of Knives

Three of Knives

Four of Knives

Five of Knives

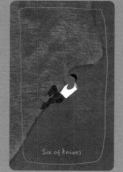

Six of Knives

Seven of Knives

Eight of Knives

KNIVES

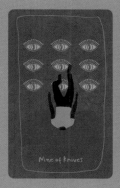
Nine of Knives

Ten of Knives

ACE OF KNIVES

Traits: Breakthrough(s), clarity

Card Description: A woman stands with a city silhouetted behind her. She holds a knife, prepared for anything headed her way. A raven flies above, showcasing its ability to survive the sun, hinting at a change in consciousness. The Ace of Knives is about stepping back into your power. The woman is headed toward new beginnings.

It is time to channel this new energy and allow it to help you in your decision-making. This card asks you to be open to different perspectives. Approach situations rationally, putting aside temptations and emotions. This new clarity may call upon you to speak your truth or voice new boundaries. Do not fear using your words or your voice.

In Yang: Seeing through illusions, facing fears, acknowledgment and acceptance of truth (even when it hurts)

In Yin: Clouded judgment, hostile and domineering individuals, making a terrible choice

Aligning: Find time to be still and silent. Listen for guidance to make wise choices.

TWO OF KNIVES

Traits: An impasse, decisions

Card Description: A woman is in dancer pose (Natarajasana); above her on the wall are two knives crossed. The woman practices mindfulness, preparing herself emotionally for any crossroads she may face. The dancer's pose is a heart-opening movement suggesting that you trust your heart over your clouded mind.

This card asks you to find balance. Be stable yet at ease, be committed but not attached, be engaged but at peace. The knives symbolize conflicting thoughts, visions, or ideas. The Two of Knives asks for patience, even if the lack of an immediate solution causes tension. Recognize that you don't know enough yet. Now is the time to get input and gather feedback.

In Yang: Deception and lies being exposed, being in touch with true feelings and being able to voice them

In Yin: Stalemate around difficult decisions, lesser of two evils, suppressed emotions, avoidance of real issues

Aligning: Rest and listen to binaural beats.

THREE OF KNIVES

Traits: Sorrow, grief

Card Description: A man sits in a chair, knitting as it rains outside. The man is working on repairing recent emotional turmoil. He was caught off guard, which led to hurt and heartbreak. There is no sugarcoating the meaning of the Three of Knives—it indicates loss, and that loss is painful.

This card asks you to release anything or anyone that is weighing your heart down, as holding on to negative energy will continue to burden the heart. The Three of Knives asks you to feel and process; understand that healing is not linear or instantaneous. Rainbows are discovered at the end of storms. You must trust that one day your wounds will be mended. We tend to forget how healing water is to our being, allowing for cleansing and growth. It is time to step outside and let the rain do its job.

In Yang: Reconciliation and forgiveness, seeking help for mental or emotional struggles, accepting an apology in your own time

In Yin: Emotional trauma or heartbreak, painful endings and goodbyes, awful news

Aligning: Personalize or organize your space in a fresh way.

FOUR OF KNIVES

Traits: Renewal, rest

Card Description: A man sits comfortably, reading and indulging in a charcuterie board. Rest is revolutionary, so make time to quiet your mind. "Doing" can be a difficult habit to break in our capitalistic world. Our need for instant gratification makes it hard to step off the hamster wheel. Take time to step away from the external and focus on the internal.

The Four of Knives reminds us of the necessity of solitude, asking us to clear blockages that are preventing inner peace. Be still and allow to surface that which needs to be shed because you have grown. It is time to retreat from the hustle. You need and deserve a break to recoup.

In Yang: Well-needed rest (of mind, body, and soul), recentering, sanctuary, quiet preparation

In Yin: Isolation and loneliness, exhaustion, rejection, misunderstanding

Aligning: Ask yourself what your immediate priority is, and set aside everything else. When the immediate tasks are handled, take a break, and then begin the next priority.

FIVE OF KNIVES

Traits: Winning at all costs, conflict

Card Description: Two individuals battle as a third watches from his throne. In this fight, there are no winners. Not even the person on the throne has gained. Onlookers watch in fear, enjoyment, and sorrow. The Five of Knives warns you not to get so lost in battle that you forget what you are fighting for. The chaos stems from a lack of communication.

The Five of Knives asks you to pick your battles. Many battles are rooted in inequitable systems and lies of scarcity created by those who benefit from us fighting among ourselves. Any pain that the individuals inflict on each other is rhythmically mirrored. Stop acting in your own self-interest; make a different choice and drop your swords. Expand your sense of self; see the larger view of who you are. Our self is our neighbor. Our self is the world. Our self is the universe.

In Yang: Conflict resolution, making amends, confrontation of evil and exposure of treachery, virtuous wrath

In Yin: Not playing nice, hinting at a loss, troublemakers, liars, haters, frenemies

Aligning: Transmute your passion and high-level energy into love, compassion, and grace. Share the love.

SIX OF KNIVES

Traits: Rite of passage, transition

Card Description: A young man is rock climbing, using knives to help him scale the face. He is ready to transition toward something new. Where are you ready to evolve? Announce it to the universe. The climb represents putting in the work to grow, and letting go of anything that encourages stagnation. Be willing and open to explore new lands and shores. You will benefit by going with the grain.

The rock climber has come a long way while working toward a brighter future. The Six of Knives reminds us that change often comes about after periods of discomfort. It is never too late to step into a new existence. Allow others to lend a hand as you work toward the top. The pack on the man's back symbolizes the weight we carry from heartbreak, conflict, or trauma. It is time to transform through healing; you have come too far to turn back now.

In Yang: Moving on and releasing all that no longer serves your higher self, entering calmer waters, new environment or atmosphere bringing much-needed relief

In Yin: Unfinished business, lack of progression, resistance to change, holding on to baggage

Aligning: Get out of your comfort zone.

SEVEN OF KNIVES

Traits: Betrayal, deception

Card Description: A man stands ready to fight. Depending on interpretation, he could be either attacking or defending. This card warns of attackers acting from a lack of conscience and making decisions that take advantage of others. Are you attacking or defending?

If you are the attacker, using manipulative behaviors to get ahead or gain the upper hand, this is your reminder that there are other, less harmful ways to attain what you would like or to accomplish what you need. If you are the defender, keep your eyes and ears to the ground, and pay close attention to whom you are keeping as close company. This card shines a light on dishonesty that is afoot, suggesting that you ensure that you and those around you are operating from a place of truth and honesty.

In Yang: Sincere apologies, coming clean, turning over a new leaf, reparations

In Yin: Lack of consciousness, moral compass has been swayed, leading to unethical behavior, imposter system, hidden agendas, shameful secrets, conspiracies

Aligning: Create an anchor. Align with your core values.

EIGHT OF KNIVES

Traits: Negativity, self-imposed restriction

Card Description: A woman looks at herself in the mirror; she is wrapped in a towel covered in knives. The knives represent the fears creating her self-made prison. Fear of failure? Fear of lack? Fear of abandonment? Fear of being alone? The fears trap us in a place of feeling powerless, confused, or lost. While the chaos and trauma that created the fear may be over, the scarring from the past experiences paralyzes you from seeing what keeps you stationary.

It is time to face what you have been avoiding. Difficult times may have taught you to doubt yourself or your mind or encouraged you to act small. The Eight of Knives is a call to reclaim your mental health. Challenge self-doubt, feeling damaged or worthless. You, like the woman, do not have to remain trapped. Work toward being whole and feeling comfortable in your own company without the weight of the towel.

In Yang: Positive inner critic, facing fears and truths, freedom

In Yin: Victim mentality, fear of failure, dark and negative thoughts

Aligning: Become a plant parent and affirm yourself and your plants daily.

NINE OF KNIVES

Traits: Anxiety, depression

Card Description: A man chooses to bury his head into his couch. He is suffering hopelessness, fear, anxiety, and despair. With his head covered, he cannot see that he is protected and safe, that he is vital and needed, that he is worthy and deserving of a whole life. This card speaks to allowing negativity to embody your whole existence, and how living in that negative emotional space leads to feeling overwhelmed, stressed, and unhappy. Although you may feel helpless to transition to a better space, that could not be further from the truth.

The Nine of Knives reminds you that you matter and are worthy of thriving, but you must see and know your whole self, honoring your shadows while understanding that you exist beyond them. Find where you are holding on to and feeding into guilt, shame, and self-loathing. Take steps to affirm your value to yourself. Your shadows are part of you, but they are not all of you.

In Yang: Asking for professional help with anxiety and/or depression, the worst of it being over, restored hope

In Yin: Darkest before dawn, mental anguish, remorse, guilt, regret

Aligning: Listen to binaural beats overnight (417Hz).

TEN OF KNIVES

Traits: Crisis, painful endings

Card Description: A woman kneels on the ground, wounded, looking up to the sky in her disheveled state. She has hit a record low, but the sun peeks through the clouds at her, hinting that not all is lost. When the woman has healed and processed her injuries— mentally, physically, and emotionally—the time for her to stand up and continue her journey will have come.

The Ten of Knives is a card of endings and closure. It's time to start over and embrace a new energy. The woman has been hurt by many weapons, where one would have been enough. While the woman's pain and suffering are sincere, she must ensure that she doesn't fall prey to a victim mentality. You have learned many lessons by this point; take that knowledge and make different choices to bring about a new outcome.

In Yang: Recovery, making it through trials and tribulations, trusting your intuition around who is *really* in your inner circle

In Yin: Rock bottom/destruction/crises, deep wounds, refusal to accept that something or someone is over

Aligning: Allow your working and living environments the chance to breathe (open the windows).

Ace of coins

Two of coins

Three of coins

Four of coins

Five of coins

Six of coins

Seven of coins

Eight of coins

COINS

Nine of coins

Ten of coins

ACE OF COINS

Traits: Abundance, new financial or career opportunity

Card Description: A woman is standing in a body of water, holding up a large cowrie shell. The shell indicates a new earthly opportunity. The opportunity will be tangible, created through physical effort and work. It is time to start planting some seeds; a new place to garden is being extended to you. Are you ready to commit to a fresh chance?

The Ace of Coins reminds you of your capacity to create, to birth, and to grow. Begin to build a foundation to shore up the process of making your dreams concrete. You can attract all you need to make your hopes and goals possible. Tap into being real and centered; regularly connect with nature to stay grounded.

In Yang: Successful manifesting, having a strong support system, fertility

In Yin: Lack of foresight, bad investments, bankruptcy, overspending, greed, materialism, miserly energy

Aligning: Write down your dreams in the present tense, as though they have already happened.

TWO OF COINS

Traits: Prioritization, adaptability

Card Description: A young man juggles two cowrie shells on a sports field. The shells here represent roles and responsibilities. The man is practicing finding his balance while holding focus in more than one area. Find balance in work, rest, relationships, exercise, and leisure. Work on creating a flow and implementing systems that will allow you to multitask with ease.

The Two of Coins encourages you to handle the unexpected with a sense of calm. Roll with the punches, and don't take them personally; be adaptable to life's challenges. While the man doesn't shy away from hard work, he knows his capacity and stays within it. You will overcome anything that comes your way if you manage your energy, time, and wealth.

In Yang: Collaboration and partnerships, adaptation, multitasking, prioritization, being in sync and in balance

In Yin: Carrying a weight that is not yours to carry, feeling financially stretched, biting off more than you can chew

Aligning: Turn off your notifications and truly "clock out" outside of work hours.

THREE OF COINS

Traits: Collaboration, implementation

Card Description: A woman is painting in her studio; creating is her "something special" that only she can bring to the world. The cowrie shells on her clothing are a reminder of the wealth that comes with collaboration. Know and appreciate that each person brings something unique to every experience. The card encourages understanding of the power of great change that can arise from joint effort. The Three of Coins is about building something tangible; it inspires meaningful and worthwhile work, projects, and creation. This kind of building takes patience and practice, as it comes with a learning curve.

Don't get discouraged if you run into setbacks or make mistakes. Understand that mastering a skill does not require you to be perfect. Mountains, hills, and potholes can be our best teachers, often in hindsight. Hold on to the passion you carry for the skills you are honing. Use the energy to prepare and plan, taking note of all the details, and your efforts will prosper. Have pride in both what you are doing and how you are getting it done.

In Yang: Improvement in social standing, exceeding expectations, goal orientation

In Yin: Misalignment, undermining projects, falling short, work-related conflict and challenges

Aligning: Host a scavenger hunt or do an escape room.

FOUR OF COINS

Traits: Conservatism, security

Card Description: A woman looks at the door expectantly. She has her cowrie shells tucked behind her back. Her shells hold the energy of earthly stability and security. This energy is different from being secure and stable in yourself. While we all want to live comfortably, material comfort and gain should not come at the expense of others. The Four of Coins warns of becoming fixated on earthly wealth and prosperity.

When you have a one-track mind around financial concerns, it is easy to become disconnected from what is truly important in life. While having savings put away for a rainy day is necessary and wise, make sure you are not operating from a scarcity mindset. A scarcity mindset is fear rooted in believing and acting from the idea that there will never be enough. The goal is to walk in the world carrying an abundance mindset, having gratitude while knowing that there is more than enough to go around. Understand that giving and receiving are not separate entities—a balancing act requires being able to receive when you give and being able to pay it forward when you graciously receive.

In Yang: Financial security, living within your means, solid budgeting

In Yin: Scarcity mindset, possessiveness, extreme conservativism with money, hoarding, controlling or clingy behavior

Aligning: Financially support something you believe in.

FIVE OF COINS

Traits: Poverty mindset, financial loss

Card Description: A man wearing summer clothes walks outside in a winter storm. His current state is not adding up with his environment, leading to this rough patch. He is operating in survival mode, which comes with feeling disadvantaged and an overwhelming sense of lack. You don't have to be financially struggling to experience poverty or scarcity consciousness. The Five of Coins asks you what you can do to change the situation.

The cowrie shells are the sign that there is a way to overcome your current hard times—sometimes that requires asking for help. Walk away from areas, people, and things that do not support you in self-improvement, healing, and growth. Do not accept suffering, pain, and fear. Work to detach yourself from the struggle.

In Yang: Light at the end of the tunnel, renewed faith and recovery, overcoming adversity with good fortune

In Yin: Poverty and exclusion as a trade-off for spiritual gain, recession, misfortune, need, homelessness, unemployment

Aligning: Take care of something that needs more nurturing or that you have been neglecting.

SIX OF COINS

Traits: Giving, sharing

Card Description: A husband and wife take the time to do their child's hair together. They are braiding her hair and adding cowrie shells. A lot is given in the act of styling hair; it is a legacy that continues as a humble labor of love. The giving of the cowrie shells symbolizes the parents passing along wealth in its many forms. The parents understand that all they offer ultimately increases their plate as well. The child is both being taught and seeing modeled the importance of community and aiding others.

The roots of welcoming others, offering food, and collaborating around resources provide the energy behind the Six of Coins. This does not mean to give and take ignorantly as a colonizer, but to give and take sustainably and equitably. We do not all have equal or equitable resources or privileges. Honor giving when you can increase opportunities for others as they build themselves, and be open to receiving when others want to help you build you.

In Yang: Financial generosity and fairness, sharing all forms of wealth with the community, bountiful sharing in abundance and without hesitation

In Yin: Disinheritance, strings attached, not set up for success

Aligning: Remember the law of giving and receiving: when you have plenty, you have plenty to share with others.

SEVEN OF COINS

Traits: Investment, sustainable results

Card Description: A woman sits on the shoreline, enjoying the tide coming in. She knows that the seeds she planted have taken root. Now is the time to rest, pause, and reflect. You have put in the hard work, dedication, and discipline; take the time to bask in your upcoming harvest. It is important to make time to honor progress while you grow, heal, build, and create.

The Seven of Coins offers congratulations on your solid foundation and celebrates your accomplishments and achievements. Contemplate your life before this point. What adversities did you work to overcome? Consider your "why." Are you still on course and getting the results you are working toward? Take pride in your perseverance, mending, and manifesting. Once you have regained your breath and feel rejuvenated, keep going.

In Yang: Enjoying the fruits of your labor, big-picture insight, accessing progress and alignment

In Yin: Fruitless endeavors, lack of rewards, work or job exploitation, giving up prematurely

Aligning: List positive life results you worked hard to achieve.

EIGHT OF COINS

Traits: Education, employment

Card Description: A woman sits at a table, engaging in a variety of forms of divination. Her passion and soul mission have led her to work on strengthening her connections to her Ancestors and their wisdom and knowledge. This card speaks of the energy of giving your all. The woman is cultivating her divination abilities, seeing how her gifts can help her as a lightworker who intends to improve the lives of others. Each time she does the same task with regularity and unwavering attention, she moves toward a new level of mastery. Paying meticulous attention to every detail, she finds her work profoundly productive and satisfying.

The Eight of Coins is a reminder to carve out time to hone your skills and talents. It is important to move beyond your comfort zone and the limitations you have set for yourself in order to evolve and see your true capabilities. Know that any energy, time, and heart you invest in your development will be worth your while.

In Yang: Production and routine, making money through skilled labor, mastery and skill development

In Yin: Perfectionism, incompetence, shortcuts, suppression, lack of inspiration and ambition

Aligning: Have a personal dance party.

NINE OF COINS

Traits: Self-sufficient, luxury

Card Description: A couple stands at the entrance of their home, welcoming guests with honey jars and figs. They have built their empire and are comfortably self-sufficient. The couple has broken free of the constructs created to limit them and now have a flourishing hive made on their terms. The two honor each other as equals and take pride in the home they have made. They are filled with gratitude for their lifestyle, circumstances, and company.

The Nine of Coins rings of abundance. The couple appreciates moving at a slower pace, taking care of their environment, and acknowledging their success. They make time to thank those who came before them, who paved the way. What is your manifesto? Continue to structure your life in a way that works for you in balance and sustainability. Feel confident in your ability to handle anything that comes your way. Trust your voice, and don't be afraid to create a path where few have wandered.

In Yang: Prosperity and comfort and having the time and state of mind to enjoy it, having resources on hand to make further gains, prosperity as a result of hard work

In Yin: Living beyond your means, caring for others for financial gain, trying to "keep up with the Joneses"

Aligning: Enhance your space. Create an environment that feels rich in the ways that matter to you.

TEN OF COINS

Traits: Generational wealth, financial security

Card Description: A family gathers together, cowrie shells strung above their heads. The family has everything they need, and there is more than enough to go around. The Ten of Coins comes with the comfort of knowing you are held. The card represents complete earthly and material success. But the card also carries the warning of becoming stagnant and complacent. Worldly wealth is not the be-all and end-all.

The family is building its legacy and knows that real wealth extends far beyond funds. They are working to leave their descendants better off than they were during their time on Earth. Take care that your resources are being used in ways that move us closer to the world you believe in. Make decisions rooted in love—for yourself, for others, and for the planet. Now that you're secure on solid ground, prepare for what comes next.

In Yang: Generational wealth, old money, legacies, family traditions and gatherings, plenty

In Yin: Rejection of roots and heritage, challenges of wealth, shameful legacies, broken families

Aligning: Write letters to everyone who's ever been important to you. Then send them or give them back to the Earth.

ABOUT THE AUTHOR

Nyasha Williams is a creator, activist, and author of the children's book *I Affirm Me: The ABCs of Inspiration for Black Kids* and of the self-published children's book *What's the Commotion in the Ocean?*

Nyasha was born in mountain time in Aurora, Colorado, and grew up living in the United States and South Africa. She received a bachelor's degree from William Jewell College and a diploma in culinary arts and wine from Prue Leith Chefs Academy. She has a master's degree in curriculum and instruction with a gifted and talented endorsement from Regent University. Nyasha lives in Northglenn, Colorado, with her husband. She is passionate about real conversations and about feeling at home in the deep end, and she loves gathering, learning, and healing with others through genuine human connection.

Nyasha pursues social justice, decolonizing work, and creating for her community full-time. Her current projects range from educator-created antiracist curriculum development to designing Ancestral money for individuals of the African diaspora. You can find her on Instagram at @writingtochangethenarrative and @decolonize_you.

ABOUT THE ILLUSTRATOR

.... 🌙 ....

Kimishka Naidoo is a multidisciplinary creative from South Africa. She studied motion picture at AFDA (South African School of Motion Picture and Live Performance). After a few years of traveling and working as a video editor and motion graphics artist, she returned to South Africa. Her love of drawing began at a young age, but it wasn't until her late twenties that she pursued illustration. It was during that time that she discovered digital illustration, and the rest is history. Today, her work centers around the unique diversity of South Africans.

Kimishka decided to work on this unique project because it aligns with her cause of expanding the representation of BIPOCs. Being given the opportunity by Nyasha to create something so beautiful and distinctive could not be passed up.